ESL
IS EVERYBODY'S
BUSINESS

ESL

IS EVERYBODY'S
BUSINESS

FRAN PARKIN ■ FELICITY SIDNELL

Pembroke Publishers Limited

© 1992 Pembroke Publishers Limited,
538 Hood Road
Markham, Ontario
L3R 3K9

Canadian Cataloguing in Publication Data

Parkin, Fran
  E.S.L. is everybody's business.

Includes bibliographical references.
ISBN 0-921217-79-X

1. English language – Study and teaching as a second language (Secondary).* 2. Mainstreaming in education. I. Sidnell, Felicity. II. Title.

PE1128.A2P37 1992   428'.0071'2   C92-093081-6

Editor: Joanne Close
Design: John Zehethofer
Typesetting Jay Tee Graphics Ltd.

Printed and bound in Canada by Webcom Limited

0 9 8 7 6 5 4 3 2

Contents

Foreward 7

Chapter 1: Raising the Profile 9
Playing Many Parts *11*
Models of Program Delivery *14*
How School Systems Have Addressed the Influx
of New Students *14*
ESL Credits and What They Mean *16*

**Chapter 2: Reception, Welcoming, and Assessment
Procedures** *21*
Topic Suggestions for a Student Handbook *22*
Reception Welcoming Centres *24*
Here's How to Do It *25*
In-School Reception and Assessment *27*
But There's No ESL Department in My School *28*
Initial Assessment of Student Writing *29*

**Chapter 3: Increasing the Comfort Level in Your
Classroom** *37*
Some First Day Strategies *38*
Strategies to Build Confidence *41*
Sample Information Form for Classroom Teachers *44*

**Chapter 4: Assisting Students to Learn a Second
Language** *45*
How We Learn A New Language *45*
A Strategy That Works: Co-operative Learning *48*
Listening *50*
Speaking *51*
Reading *52*
Writing *53*

Chapter 5: Program Planning and Adaptation 55
Collaborative Curriculum Planning 56
Using Students' Experiences to Create Curriculum 57
Taking Down the Walls 58
Education for Social Justice 59
Anxiety Attacks/Curriculum Angst 59
Language Across the Curriculum 60
Modifying a Science Lesson 62

Chapter 6: Evaluating Students 65
Observation is the Key 65
How to Evaluate 67
Implications for Designing Assignments and Courses 67

Chapter 7: Responding to Issues 71
The Challenge for the Teacher 71
Students Speak Out 71
Parents as Partners 72
Issues Raised by Teachers 72
Issues Raised by Students 76
Issues Raised by Parents and the Community 78

Chapter 8: Building Commitment 83
Sharing Ownership 83
Developing a Language Policy for the Whole School 84
Drawing Up a School-Based Needs Assessment 84
Reflecting the Principles of Anti-Racist Education 86
Extending the Commitment 87
System-Wide Initiatives 87
Political Action 88
Background Information on Student Population
of the School 90
Background Survey of Teaching and Non-Teaching Staff
of the School 91

Bibliography 93

Foreword

Recently, the need has intensified for practical materials that will assist teachers whose students vary greatly in educational background. The successful mainstreaming of students who are still learning English as their second language is a key concern for many teachers. In large cities, such students have made up a significant proportion of the student body for a number of years. Moreover, in recent years, a population spread has resulted in the enrollment of considerable numbers of such students in suburban boards.

As a result, teachers who may have little or no background in ESL can be faced with the task of teaching Science, Mathematics, Geography or History to a diverse group of students, some of whom are still learning to communicate in English. In addition to the language factor, some students may have major gaps in their formal education that cannot be ignored by core subject teachers. In both instances, these young people are adjusting to new situations and systems, and need support and encouragement to build on their previous knowledge and experience.

What do these students bring to the classroom? They bring a wealth of experience that can be shared with their teachers and classmates. As teachers draw on this, seeking out and including in the curriculum materials from other cultures which may be familiar to them, the study of a subject is enriched for all students. The real challenge for the teacher is to find ways for the class to share in the richness offered by the presence of students from other cultures and countries.

It is important that academic programs be examined in light of present thinking about how students learn, with particular reference to new students arriving from other cultures and countries. Many ESL methodologies can be brought to bear on course content in core subject areas. ESL teachers must re-evaluate their aims and objectives in situations where integration of curriculum is important. Core subject curriculums must be re-examined, modified, and adapted to meet the needs of students who demonstrate a wide variety of educational backgrounds and language skills. This book, then, is addressed to teachers, administrators, consultants, and support staff in middle and secondary schools. We hope that some of its suggestions will be helpful.

The authors wish to thank Freda Appleyard, Linda Hart-Hewins, and Zig Parkin for their helpful suggestions for the manuscript's improvement, Christine Yee and Angela Goyeau for their assistance, and all the students whose stories contributed to the development of the book.

CHAPTER 1

Raising the Profile

In recent years, global issues have precipitated an unprecedented mobility among the world's populations. As a result, increasing numbers of immigrant, refugee, and visa students from a wide range of backgrounds, cultures, languages, and dialects are enrolling in schools in their new homelands. In large metropolitan areas, the number of students in, or graduated from, ESL programs may make up the majority of the school population.

The presence of these students in a school brings with it the possibility of many benefits for students, teachers, the school as a whole, and ultimately, society. Such newly-arrived students may have had years of formal education, and may even have professional qualifications or university degrees. They bring their culture with them, and the knowledge they have gained from the variety of experiences they have lived through. The diversity of culture and experience that these students represent can enrich classroom learning for all students. Furthermore, teachers will have access to a unique resource in these students to expand and enrich curriculum. The whole school can become a multicultural community that inculcates tolerance for, and understanding of, all cultures. Finally, when these students graduate, they will be ready to make a significant contribution to their new society.

In addition, the limited language facility of these students can be a positive force, stimulating and challenging teachers and educational systems. These students are of all ages and have diverse academic, social, cultural, and linguistic needs. Some students may have had an interrupted education and will need opportunities to catch up, while others may speak another language or dialect of English at home and may not yet have acquired the proficiency in English needed for success in an academic setting. In order to address these varying needs, educators will need to re-examine curricula and course goals, provide resources to support and extend the curriculum, and develop in-service training for teachers. Teachers will need to explore new methodologies, adapt and develop materials, and at times create curriculum. The results will be mutually rewarding for you and your students. You, as a teacher or an administrator, now have the opportunity to make a difference for these students.

To begin, you will need to be aware of a number of factors that typify these students and influence their success. Without such an understanding, it will be difficult to respond effectively to their needs.

Be aware that these students are not only coping with the demands that are placed on other students, but may also have additional stresses that can have a bearing on their academic success. As a result, demands will be placed on both your sensitivity and resourcefulness to ensure that such students meet with success, in spite of these difficulties.

What are some of the stresses that could be experienced by your students?

- Some may be adults who find themselves placed in classes largely composed of adolescents.
- Students may frequently move from school to school during the course of the school year, resulting in a lack of continuity in their educational experience.
- Students from small, rural settings may experience a form of culture shock when they move to large, urban centres.
- Students may live on their own and experience extreme loneliness and isolation.

- Students may live under adverse conditions, work long hours, have the responsibilities of a single parent, live in crowded quarters, and cope with poverty.
- Students may have little or no knowledge of possible career opportunities and therefore find it difficult to establish future goals for themselves.
- Many students may feel insecure about their status in the country because of long and complicated immigration procedures.
- Students may miss blocks of school time while they deal with their legal status and family responsibilities.
- If students have been separated from their parents, they may have to assume the role of a parent for a younger sibling or experience a reversal of roles in the family, since they have some facility in English.
- Many students may suffer from the traumatic effects of war or the dangers of escape from their homeland.
- Students may experience anxiety and fear because they have left family members behind in their country or in refugee camps.
- Students may find themselves under extreme pressure to succeed because their families have sacrificed everything to send them away. This burden of guilt may cause some students to work at a full-time job, in addition to attending school, in order to be self-supporting and to send some money to assist their families.

What, then, are some of the implications of these circumstances for you as their classroom teacher?

Playing Many Parts

By now you probably realize that you are in a position where you can make a major difference in the lives of your students. Your teaching repertoire must include the good teaching practices associated with effective learning. In addition, you will assume new roles in your teacher-student relationships.

- Your flexibility and ability to adapt to changes in your classes will be of primary importance. This flexibility will be vital in such areas as: choice of appropriate materials, grouping of students, modification of curriculum, ability to alter lessons in mid-stream, and setting of deadlines for assignments (the tyranny of being too rigid will create barriers between you and your students, resulting in mutual frustration, student failure, and dropouts).
- You will need to make a concerted effort to get to know your students. Develop an awareness of their circumstances and their needs so that you don't misjudge them or jump to wrong conclusions. As an example, failure to have homework done may not be the result of laziness or indifference, but the result of having a full-time job after school.
- Build up a rapport with your students by speaking to them personally or by encouraging them to write about themselves. In addition, by tuning in to what students say to each other, you may be surprised by what you learn about their lives. Show a personal interest in your students: inspire their trust and confidence so that they will talk to you more openly.
- You will need to show sensitivity and understanding toward the students. Your primary concern is for their welfare, not for whether your assignment has been completed or an arbitrary deadline has been met. Above all, be fair and be prepared to give your students the benefit of the doubt. Remember that they need positive feedback and reassurance, just as you would if you were faced with major changes in your life. You can't over-encourage your students.
- In cases where your students have gaps in the continuity of their education or may unavoidably miss major blocks of your course because of personal circumstances, establish support mechanisms such as pairing them with learning partners. Peer support or tutoring arrangements in which students share notes, review missed material, or get assistance with difficult topics can be mutually

beneficial. As well, try to find time to be available to your students outside of class time.

- As a classroom teacher, you may find yourself developing a multiple personality, since you will be taking on roles of substitute parent, advisor, sympathetic listener, guidance counsellor, advocate, or social worker. You may be the only adult in some of your students' lives — you can provide them with an adult perspective. You may have to help them deal with government, welfare, and health care systems, all of which can be confusing and intimidating. You may find yourself assisting them in filling out a myriad of forms and translating legal jargon. In your classroom, be prepared to offer some career counselling when needed. Provide your students with possible career goals and positive role models by inviting former successful students to speak to your students.
- Where you have observed that your students are in need of financial aid for clothing, food, housing or school supplies, find out where to get assistance in your community. Some schools provide a clothing depot or conduct food drives for needy families.

All these demands and expectations may seem overwhelming. They needn't be. Remember that your continued awareness of these factors in your day-to-day activities will inevitably influence the effectiveness of your classes and make a difference to your students. Your reward is the direct feedback from students and tangible proof that you are having an effect on their lives. What can be more rewarding for a teacher than seeing that what you are doing counts?

Now that you have arrived at an understanding of the students you will be working with, and the many parts you may be required to play, the question of suitable program delivery arises.

Models of Program Delivery

Models of program delivery vary from system to system and from school to school. The choice of program may depend on the number of students requiring language support within the board or within a particular school, and on the number of staff available to provide support.

In schools where the ESL enrollment is small, students are generally placed according to age and educational background, and integrated into mainstream classrooms where they receive linguistic support in multi-ability groupings. Gradually, these students' language proficiency increases as they interact with their English-speaking peers. With the sensitive support of the teacher and the help of other students, this can be an excellent way to learn the language. Students acquire language holistically by participating actively in purposeful classroom activities that require them to listen, speak, read, and write in an interrelated way. Through engagement in student-centred tasks, they begin to find meaning by experiencing and using language to communicate with others.

In schools that receive larger numbers of students requiring language support, separate ESL courses and special sections of subject classes may be offered. If this is the case, administrators must give careful attention to the positioning of ESL classes and special sections of subject classes in the timetable so that classes do not conflict. Programming and timetabling must be flexible if schools are to adapt to the changing needs of students. As students' facility in English increases at different rates, there will be movement in and out of ESL classes when students are integrated into mainstream classes. This can be a challenge for the timetabler.

How School Systems Have Addressed the Influx of New Students

The following are some of the current programming practices found in many school systems:

14

Intensive Support Program

Intensive programs are provided for students who have very limited or no knowledge of English, and who may require upgrading in basic literacy skills because of an uneven educational background. Courses concentrate on the development of the basic communication skills of listening, speaking, reading and writing, and on orientation to the students' new environment. Secondary school students receive academic credits for these courses. Students may be timetabled for half the school day into classes offered by the ESL department, which usually includes ESL 1 (First Course) and a life skills course. This arrangement allows students to learn about their new society as they are learning the language, and enables them to earn additional elective credits. For the remainder of the day, students may be placed in special sections of other subject courses where the language demands are such that they can participate actively and experience success. Such courses might include Mathematics, Art, Music, Keyboarding, and Physical Education.

Partial Support Program

In this model, common to many schools, students may be timetabled into separate ESL classes at the ESL 2, 3, and 4 (Second, Third, Fourth Courses) levels of proficiency. These classes usually extend over a number of years while the students still require ongoing language support. It should be noted that not all students will work through the levels. You will find that some students are able to move from Level 2 to Level 4, from Level 3 to total integration, and so on. At the ESL 2 level, students may spend one-third of the school day in ESL classes, while at the ESL 3 and 4 levels, they may take concurrently one class of ESL and another of English as a bridge to the mainstream. They will gradually spend increased time attending a broad variety

---

NOTE: ESL 1, 2, 3, 4, designations refer to level of proficiency in English, not to grade level.

of mainstream classes at different grade levels, sometimes in special sections of the subject, and sometimes completely integrated into the mainstream. These classes might include Geography, History, Computer Studies, Science, and Technological Studies.

Tutorial Support Program

Students who have achieved an advanced level of fluency may be integrated fully into mainstream classes, receiving ESL support, when needed, from an ESL or resource teacher. This person, in collaboration with the mainstream classroom teacher, can analyze the language demands of the subject area and help to design, modify, and deliver a suitable program in the mainstream classroom. In some schools, ESL support may be offered to small groups of students inside the mainstream classroom, while in other schools, students may be withdrawn individually or in small groups for tutoring by ESL staff. As well, students may be available as peer tutors to offer additional support in or out of the class. The benefits to both learning partners of peer tutoring are considerable; the tutor consolidates understanding of a concept or topic through organizing and explaining thoughts coherently; the second-language learner gains linguistic and academic proficiency, and self-confidence from a peer who can serve as a role model.

ESL Credits and What They Mean

What should a classroom teacher expect if a student is studying at the ESL 1, 2, 3, or 4 level?

The following brief descriptions are provided to assist classroom teachers to formulate expectations for students in each of the levels of ESL. Remember, language learning requires time: research indicates that it may take more than five years to learn a language fluently. Because there are wide differences among students, teachers will need to be patient as students proceed at their own pace through the process. And while courses proceed in a continuum, it must be understood that some students may change levels during the school year, or may skip levels on the recommendation of their ESL teacher.

ESL 1

Students placed in a first-year ESL course have little or no knowledge of English. Some may still be learning the Roman alphabet or adapting to reading from left to right. By the end of their first course, however, they should be able to respond to short questions, follow simple instructions, communicate immediate needs, or carry on a short conversation in English. In fact, they may understand a great deal more than they are able to express, either verbally or in writing. Their comprehension, however, will be greatly enhanced if spoken or written lessons are supplemented with concrete materials or demonstrations.

ESL 2

Students at the ESL 2 level have studied English previously, and may be able to participate with some fluency and confidence in small group activities in the classroom. By the end of this course, they may be able to give brief oral reports, take notes, and complete written assignments with relative accuracy. Some may need help with reading comprehension while others may be beginning to read independently, and may be able to make inferences, state opinions, make judgments, and draw conclusions. Some students may experience difficulty understanding oral presentations and class discussions, and may require assistance in completing reading and writing assignments. Others will be capable of writing for a variety of purposes and audiences, and will be increasingly able to self-correct their written work.

ESL 3

Students at the ESL 3 level can participate meaningfully in most mainstream subject classes. By the end of this course, students should be able to understand and use language in a variety of circumstances with increasing confidence and complexity. They will read with increasing fluency, using skimming and scanning techniques, respond to authentic, unabridged texts and materials, and will be able to write in a variety of modes. They should be able to research information with assistance and express themselves, verbally and in writing, in complex language.

ESL 4

Students at the ESL 4 level are practising language skills intensively to support them in senior English classes. By the end of this level, students should exhibit oral fluency, read with speed and comprehension, and be able to summarize notes. They should be able to analyze and respond to authentic literature in a variety of genres, support a thesis with logical arguments, write in informal and formal styles, and complete research projects with help from teachers and library resource personnel.

A student writes...

I COME TO CANADA FOUR YEAR AGO BECAUSE MO PERENTS WANTED COME TO VISIT. ONCE WHEN WE WERE HERE WE LIKED IT EVER MUCH DIDN'T WONT TO DO BACK TO PORTUGAL.
SO THEN WE STAYED HERE AS VISITORS FOR 3 YEARS WITH THE IMMIGRATIONS PERMISSIOR. MO FAMILLO DECIDED TO DO THE IMMIGRATIONS PERMISSIOR WE WAITED AND WAITED THE IMMIGRATIONS PAPERS AND SENDE ELLGAL IMMIGRATS BACK TO WERE THEY COME FROM.
THEM MACE THE FAMILI AND I WENT BACK TO PORTUGAL AND WE DID IMMIGRATIONS PAPER THERE.
AFTER SIX MONTHS OF WAITING WE FAMILLO BECAME LEGAL IMMIGRATS AND WE WENT BACK TO CANADA WHERE WE WERE HOPPG.
I WOLD LIKE TO GO TO SCHOOL AND PERSUE A CAREER IN ELECTRONICS.

Possible Course Progression in ESL

Suitable Options for Students at Each Level

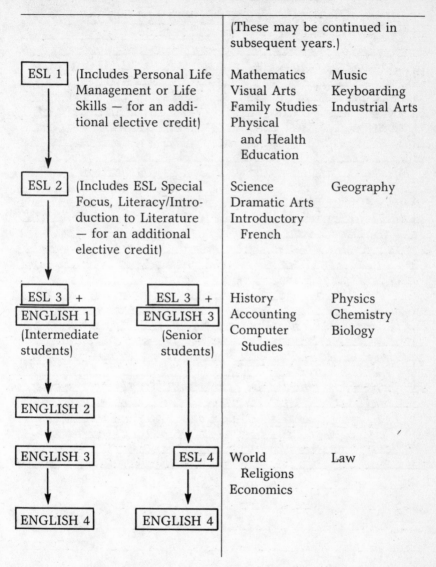

Possible Course Progression in ESL	Suitable Options for Students at Each Level
	(These may be continued in subsequent years.)
ESL 1 (Includes Personal Life Management or Life Skills — for an additional elective credit)	Mathematics, Music, Visual Arts, Keyboarding, Family Studies, Industrial Arts, Physical and Health Education
ESL 2 (Includes ESL Special Focus, Literacy/Introduction to Literature — for an additional elective credit)	Science, Geography, Dramatic Arts, Introductory French
ESL 3 + **ENGLISH 1** (Intermediate students) / **ESL 3** + **ENGLISH 3** (Senior students)	History, Physics, Accounting, Chemistry, Computer Studies, Biology
ENGLISH 2	
ENGLISH 3 / **ESL 4**	World Religions, Law, Economics
ENGLISH 4 / **ENGLISH 4**	

NOTE: At the ESL 3 and ESL 4 levels, students should be able to succeed in most mainstream courses.

A student writes. . .

My first days in a Canadian school

I was very excited can come to Toronto. I had never been abroad before. But on week I must came to school, high-school, a Canadian high school.

Different language and people make up this school like as a big family. That was the first time I found how small I was. Oh, I can not remenber anything about the first day. I had no feeling on that day. I did not feel hot, or cold. Was I like a stone. No, stones are non-living. I was a little bit "better than stone. Now I tell you I was just "dead" during the day. I was a "corpse".

After some days I could say a little English. I was so poor with my expression. I wanted to talk with other students. I got very surprise they could not understand my English. I always feel my English pronounciation was very criterion.

Up til now I have more Chinese friends than Canadian friends. I was try to do some thing with them but they did not mind me. My work usually was study. When some students went to find a job in summer I just had lessons in summer school or read a book at home.

Now I think I can listen, speak and write in English. But not very well. I can sure the teacher saying. After some time I think can be well.

Those were my first day in out school—Harbord Collegiate Institute.

CHAPTER 2

Reception, Welcoming, Assessment and Placement Procedures

Procedures to welcome, assess, and place immigrant students vary greatly. In places where the enrollment of newcomers is small, newcomers and local students may be treated the same way. The institution of a special process, however, can be helpful to families, encourage them to maintain contact with the school, and significantly ease the students' settlement in their new programs.

In an ideal situation, families or students who are on their own would be welcomed and interviewed in their own language. This is possible if there are teachers or other staff on hand who are multilingual. At other times, students at the school may be able to help with translation during the initial interviews so that families can get a better idea of school procedures. Usually, there is so much demand for the services of translators attached to school boards that it is not possible to involve them in the initial reception of new families.

Small things, however, can make a difference to the degree of welcome experienced by new students. Bulletin boards in the hall or office displaying greetings in languages from around the world, and other students' work in their heritage languages may help newcomers to feel at home. A school handbook for students and parents translated into languages common to the school population will ensure that all are able to become familiar with school structures and routines. If this is too large a project and the population is too diverse to make it financially possible, consider designing a one- or two-page flyer that contains essential information needed by the new students. Have the pages translated into a greater range of languages. As a long-term project, ask students to design and write a handbook for newcomers; this can be a very successful writing project and its product a helpful and welcoming resource for new students. Another excellent way to communicate information about the school is to make a video, showing classroom, social service and administrative activities, as well as school events. Students may provide voice overs in several languages.

Whether reception procedures are carried out within an individual school, in a department that serves several schools, or in a centre that receives all new students to the system, all procedures have the same objectives. These are: to welcome newcomers; to provide information about the schools and the school system; to inform families about programs suited to the students, given their strengths and needs; and to give the students confidence that they can succeed in the program they and their parents have chosen. The process must be designed to provide enough information about the students to be helpful to the school and their future teachers.

Topic Suggestions for a Student Handbook

1. A welcome from the principal
2. A map of the school
3. A calendar of important events including holidays
4. Getting to know the school
   What are: school hours
            home form procedures
            attendance procedures
            notes for absences
            late admit slips
            library hours?

How to get: books and supplies
a locker
gym equipment
a student transit card
financial assistance
5. Understanding the timetable
6. Understanding the ESL program
7. Understanding the requirements for graduation
8. How students are evaluated
9. Tutorial and extra help services
10. How to get help:
guidance and counselling services
translation service and translators
health services
11. How to study
12. The student council
what is a student activity card?
13. School clubs, activities, and organizations
14. How to join a team
15. Field trips
16. Summer school/night school

The reception process should increase students' and parents' understanding of the school system by involving them in decisions about placement. Successful settlement in an appropriate program is assisted by a full discussion of the students' goals, the work they have done in the assessment classrooms, and the programs that would best cater to their needs. This may require the services of an interpreter. Often, families provide such help by bringing an English-speaking relative or friend. This aids the initial assessment of the students' needs, and ensures that families and students understand the nature of the program students are entering. If it is not possible to have a translator present at the initial and subsequent placement interviews, try to arrange for a board interpreter to attend a meeting with the student and the family as soon as possible. At that time, it will be possible to check on information previously gathered in English and to explain procedures thoroughly.

The role played by the assessment process can also help students to make an initial transition from one school culture to another. Students in senior elementary or secondary schools have acquired a significant part of their education in their own countries. Even when students have had their schooling interrupted, their education has continued as a result of their experiences, whether in a job, on the street, in a camp, at home, in another country, or in flight. Students need to feel that their cultural and personal identity is respected, and that what they have learned in the past will be of value to them in the future. They need counselling about how the educational system works, what they need to do to fulfil their goals, the special support offered to learners of English, and social services available to them, including those provided by cultural organizations.

Reception Welcoming Centres

When the numbers of new students warrant it, Reception Welcoming Centres, where students of all ages are counselled and helped to enroll in suitable courses, can provide an excellent service. Reception Centres have resources to:

- Register incoming students and record their immigration and educational documents;
- Initiate a student profile containing personal information and educational history for all newly-registered students;
- Gather information concerning all elementary-school aged students that will provide a basis for ongoing assessment at their new school;
- Conduct a comprehensive assessment of students 12 years of age and older;
- Provide counselling to students and families about the school system and the programs offered;
- Arrange for the placement of students in an appropriate school and program;
- Provide information about community support services

such as health clinics, legal services, family counselling, daycare, and welfare.

Assessment is a continual process that helps to build on students' existing skills and strengths. It will be an important part of the teaching/learning process after the students have been placed in their permanent classrooms. However, Centres can provide a detailed and comprehensive report based on several days' observation of students' ability to learn, communicate and use language, and understand and apply mathematical concepts. In addition, students can be observed for their socialization and adjustment patterns, and for their response to different learning styles.

Here's How To Do It

Assessment procedures should not be an examination or a test. Formal standardized testing is not appropriate because it is often culture bound, and provides information about what students don't know rather than what they do know. Students should be able to work at their own pace and may spend four or five days in the Centre. Whenever possible, informal first language assessment should be employed, as well as assessment in English. This first language assessment enables teachers to gather information about students and their previous education, to enquire into their first language literacy skills, and to increase students' confidence and raise the comfort level during assessment.

The principles of dynamic assessment, which suggest test/teach/test procedures, can be utilized to establish what students know, as well as their response to teaching situations and different learning styles. Such procedures should be conducted in an informal classroom climate in which individual attention is paid to students so that work is done in an unstressful atmosphere. Students need encouragement to ask questions and discuss their work, and should be prompted by the teacher if necessary. In these circumstances, opportunities can be given for students' strengths

25

and weaknesses to emerge. Several lessons may be taught to gain further indication of their academic potential.

Assessment should be as interactive and informal as possible, and aim to help students to appreciate their achievements and skills, to recognize their needs, and to feel more confident of their ability to cope in a strange system. If the process begins with a personal interview, which is informal and casual, the student will not be intimidated. During the interview, the student's aural/oral skills can be assessed and insight gained into the appropriate level to begin reading and writing assessment. Choose materials that are similar to those currently in use in classrooms, for example, excerpts from school texts, as well as a variety of multicultural readings that will be familiar and meaningful to the students. If assessment focuses on comprehension, students can be given progressively more advanced material until they encounter some difficulty. All students, except those at the early beginner level, can be asked to write a composition; the more advanced students, to write a second piece that will assist in a more accurate assessment of their writing skills. Thus, students will have attempted several kinds of writing during the assessment, including responses to reading, oral discussion, personal writing and, if capable, a more formal composition on an abstract topic.

Assessment in Mathematics will give an indication of how much students know and can recall; however, the focus of the assessment should be on skills and problem-solving that do not require much language, and that will give students opportunities to show *how* they approach problems, apply knowledge, and use information. Given that many newcomers have significant gaps in their education, assessment tools need to include manipulative materials, practical problem-solving exercises, and numeracy indicators.

Work given to the students should include completed examples so that they have a chance to recall processes they have learned in the past, or to show that they can grasp a concept when presented visually. Assignments must be discussed and teaching done to check whether students can follow verbal instructions, demonstrations, and explanations. If the process is interactive and non-threatening, it is possible to gain an indication of how students learn, attack problems, make use of resources, and build relationships with others. These are important factors in the students' adaptation to mainstream classrooms.

Anecdotal reporting reflects the detailed observations of the teacher over several days. Suggestions should be made for placement. These reports will be discussed with the student by a guidance counsellor and sent with the student's work to the receiving school. The complete package will become part of a student's record. A second copy of the summary report can be sent to the teachers of the new student.

In-School Reception and Assessment

In Centres such as the type described, it is possible to have students assessed by teachers of Mathematics and a full range of materials developed to cover the needs of a varied clientele. Assessment done in the school setting, preparatory to initial placement, should also include Mathematics if possible. Many factors, such as the students' language proficiency, willingness to take part in an active learning process, age and experience, may influence their chances of success in a placement. The engagement of more than one department in the assessment of new students in a secondary school is of value because it strengthens interdepartmental collaboration; all departments are encouraged to take responsibility for the success of students who are in the process of learning English.

Although time consuming, individual assessment of new students, in which attention is paid to their communicative competence and potential to learn, is of great importance to their settlement in suitable courses and to their ultimate success. Placement should be tentative; students should be aware that it will be reviewed and that changes can be made if the placement is unsuitable.

This emphasis on the tentative nature of the placement becomes all the more important if the initial assessment procedures are conducted under pressure, in the last few days before school opens, or in the first weeks of term. At this time, schools can be inundated with an unexpected flood of new students that must be assigned to classes as soon as possible. If this is the case, make clear to the students that placement will be reviewed after a specific length of time. Point out to the teacher that the students will require further assessment during the first few weeks in the classroom. Place the students in classes where you feel confident they can cope so that should they need to be moved later, it can be a promotion rather than a demotion.

Collecting assessment tools for use on a regular basis is helpful, but more crucial is the need to develop an assessment procedure that is flexible, practical, and illuminating. The process should aim to build students' confidence and welcome them into the program. It should provide teachers with information about the students, particularly about their educational background, goals, strengths, present facility in English, and preferred learning styles.

But There's No ESL Department in My School!

In schools where there is no ESL department, you may have to place the student when s/he registers. If possible, place the student in a class with others of the same age. Have classroom teachers assess the student's proficiency and progress over the first few weeks. If you are unable to have an ESL program, consider helping your students within the mainstream classroom. While the numbers who need help may be small, this ensures that students do not miss what is going on in some subjects. Or, you may decide that a withdrawal program would suit a small group of students better. Give students as much help as possible in making an adjustment to your school. Students learn a great deal from their peers, so encourage other students to make friends. Appoint one student to be the newcomer's "buddy". Investigate the possibility of getting tutors for the student, one who will help the student learn English and another who can teach the student in his/her own language. In your classroom, you can give the student extra academic help. Of equal or greater importance is the social support you give that will ease the student's entry into the new environment.

Initial Assessment of Student Writing

When faced with the task of the initial placement of students, one of your assessment strategies will be to ask the students to produce a writing sample. Typically, the students would be asked to write on a topic to which they can relate, such as school in their country, a description of themselves or a family member, an unforgettable event, or instructions to make something. Students should not be limited by length or time restrictions — they write as much as they want. Students should also be free to make use of a standard English or bilingual dictionary. Remember that what the students produce is essentially a first draft. Evaluate their writing by using a holistic approach. This means that you read the samples rapidly in order to gain an overall impression of the students' ability to communicate. Such an approach to grading places an emphasis on students' thinking processes and clarity of expression. Of lesser importance are grammatical form and spelling which can be problematical for these students. Therefore, students' ideas, and the clarity and coherence with which they have been expressed, should be especially significant in making your assessment. However, also consider the amount of time the students took to produce the passages, their length and complexity, the variety of sentence structure, and paragraphing. Sometimes, your decision on placement will also depend on the age of the students, the number of years they will likely spend in secondary school, and the time of the students' arrival during the school year.

The following writing samples are examples of passages written for assessment purposes. The samples have been selected as being representative of writing abilities. They may assist you in making initial assessments, since the samples illustrate proficiency at each of the four levels.

I ONE DAY AN PLAY FoToBoL SAME AN PLAY TO GooD AD GoE KicKE--AD BReCK MAE LEG.
I SETAE 3 MoNTh HosTiTAL.

ESL 1 (Early)

- This student knows enough English to convey some basic information; however, the ideas are very rudimentary. The writer is stating a few simple facts with no development or descriptive details.
- The student required a long period of time to produce a very short passage.
- The student has little idea about sentence form, and does not have a good grasp of the relationship between sound and script.
- The script would indicate that the writer is not accustomed to writing in English, perhaps because the alphabet is unfamiliar, or because the writer has not had much formal practice.

How to Play Soccer

In MY country we have a Different Sports one of the Best Game is Soccer.

Soccer means Between Two Team of 11 players who kick or head a round Ball without using the arms or Hands. except The Gollkipper.

Since when I was Boy I play soccer When you play soccer you Need Soccer Shose sortpaints and Soccer Ball

Soccer very Inportant for you Health Because when you play soccer your Boody get excerice

That's why I Love to play Soccer.

ESL 1 (Late)

- The writer generated a longer passage. It indicates a more mature level of thinking and greater facility with the language.
- There is structure to the passage; there is a beginning, a middle, and an end. The student has developed the topic with a series of related ideas that have a focus. The student shows an awareness of paragraphing.
- The writer is able to convey meaning clearly, although the form of certain words may not be standard.
- The passage shows that there is some understanding of how sentences are constructed, although some of the sentence structure is faulty. Little attention is paid to punctuation.
- There is an understanding of phonetics, which allows the student to approximate the form of the words, even when their spelling is unknown.

How to learn a language

Some people afraid about another langkage. But my idea, no thing is difficult if you have a courage. First thing to learn anything you should must have courage.

Then you need good helper because without helper you cannot learn properly. For example you want to learn English. First step all time you try to speak English, go to School for learning English. You watch English programes go to market alone for shopping. on T.V

If you don't understand. asked another person. Don't feel shy. If you have confidence you learn fast. Try to correct our conversation

English is very nice language. Don't worry about it. Try keep Countinues. one day, you will speak. write and read well. But you need more practice. you listen English news and programes with been interest. If you do anything I hope,

with interest. you will find it.

ESL 2

- This student has generated a longer passage in which the ideas are expanded more fully.
- The student expresses clear ideas and is able to develop them in an organized fashion, ending with a logical conclusion.
- The passage is more effective because of the sentence variety and understanding of paragraphing.
- The student requires practice with grammatical forms, verb tenses, the use of articles, and sentence structure.
- The student is familiar with cursive script.

My self

The most familiar person to me should be myself, so I would like to talk what kind of people I really am. People often hardly read me in short time, because I am used to be quiet and rarely talk too much about myself, especialy in front of stranger; therefore, ~ the first impression I leave on people is my quiet nature.

In China, most people prefer quiet, modest and polite person to aggressive and arrogant one. Particularly a good nature is very important to a lady. for instance, A young gentlemen chooses a ideal wife in terms of her nature.

I have possessed this advantage since I was a little girl. I had never fought with my school mates. My teachers often commended me in the class and my parents were very proud of me. With growing up. I still keep my quiet nature, either studying in university or working in the hospital. On one hand because of the influence of traditional chinese culture; On another hand, the reason is one thing which I had experienced made a lasting impression on me when I worked in a hospital.

ESL 3

- This student has produced a longer, more sophisticated passage in which there is an awareness of overall structure. The passage has a definite opening that is developed in the following paragraphs; however, there is no sense of an ending.
- The paragraphs show a general unity; topic sentences are developed in the paragraphs.
- There is good variety in the sentence structure.
- The ideas are complex; however, the syntax is awkward at times.
- There is a good command of vocabulary and punctuation.

It's hard to talk about ourselves nowadays, specially if it's asked something like who you are... people can think you are egocentric, selfish, etc. just because you write down your best qualities and any "faults" (of course, you don't want them to know yours "little mistakes" and it's also pretty hard to accept it!")

However, right now I am supposed to explain for you, reader, who I am. I've got to tell you that inside of me, I am screaming "Hey boy, do I really have to go through that?"

Anyway, you must know first of all that I am a woman — or a girl? — and I am not in my twenties or thirties! I'm just seventeen... ok I admit, I am a girl! And I am not so tall as I would like to be; I'm luck I don't want to be a model! I have brown hair on my shoulders, honey-green eyes (sometimes when I like to change it to blue, I just wear my contact lenses) and my lips are as Kim Basinger does have; but I didn't make a plastic surgery!

You may be saying that this job is easy. Where is the big deal! It's just look at me!, it's not so hard to talk about yourself!!

On the other hand, the worse is coming. It means: personality. Do you really want my profile?! Ok! Briefly, I am intelligent, smart, open mind, intellectual... let's kidding! Well, I am interested in music, movies, operas, ballets and sports (I do exercices!)

I love an interestining conversation about politics, maybe I will study political science! I really like history, studies about old societies (Do you believe in the lost society of Atlanta?) and the contemporaries.

Once, a friend said that I am like a treasure box; perhaps you won't find silver or steel in, but as he said, just a golden girl.

P.S.: I also do like mysticism, and I can read your mind about being self-fish, centre of the world...

ESL 4

- This student has more facility in English and is able to generate more sophisticated ideas. She has developed a voice in her writing, exhibiting a real playfulness with the language. She is clearly aware of her audience; an interplay is established between the writer and the reader.
- The language is used in more interesting ways; there is humor and variety of sentence structure.
- The student is able to use rhetorical devices and connecting ideas, adding emphasis to what she is saying.
- The passage is cohesive.
- There are still problems with writing mechanics.

CHAPTER 3

Increasing the Comfort Level in Your Classroom

Do you remember that September-is-coming feeling? The nervous expectation on the morning of the return to school? All new beginnings set our adrenalin flowing to some extent. A current focus on the transitions students make from one school to another, and the difficulties some students have in making those transitions, have alerted us to the importance of establishing a positive, supportive classroom environment for a wide range of students. We need short-term strategies to ease the students' passage into new routines and expectations and activities to make them feel at home. Similarly, we need long-term strategies that will have a significant effect on their success. When a student faces the problems of a new classroom—unsure of what is being said, ignorant of what is expected in the classroom, and afraid of rejection and failure—starting in a new school can be a traumatic experience.

Although we all suffer to some degree from feelings of alienation and fear, we do not always recognize these emotions in others. Often, we do not know how to address these problems effectively the moment they arise, in spite of the fact that we know they hinder student progress and learning in the classroom. How can we help new students, whose English is limited, to feel at home in the classroom and to become engaged in the learning process?

First, give some thought to the possibility that your new students may have educational backgrounds that differ greatly from the majority of students in your class. Young refugees have often had minimal formal schooling. Others have had their education seriously interrupted. Knowledge has sometimes been acquired second hand, from a fellow student who was able to attend a camp school. In the case of students who received direct instruction, this may have consisted of a course in basic English only. Other students will have studied for several years in a country of first refuge, where they may have already acquired a second language that may not be English. Yet other students arrive in our schools from school systems that are very different from our own. They will, in addition to learning a new language, have to adapt to a new educational system.

Student-teacher relations in other countries are frequently very formal. Students may be accustomed to a teacher-directed classroom, considerable rote learning, and tests on the material studied. They may have learned to read by the alphabetic method, or be unfamiliar with the Roman script and still be struggling to read in English. In their culture, asking questions may have been discouraged and looked upon as a sign of disrespect to the teacher. Many immigrant students, used to very structured teaching and learning, need time to adjust to the ways of our classrooms.

Some initial steps that will help new students to become comfortable in the classroom can be taken on the first day.

Some First Day Strategies

- Welcome your new students individually to your class. That moment of acknowledgement, even if it consists only of a greeting, will help the students to feel they belong.
- Check the students' names with them so that you call them by the customary part of their full name, and have the correct pronunciation. As examples, Vietnamese students are often called by their second given name, while Spanish-speaking students pronounce "J" as "H".
- If available, read the information sheet about the students (see pg. 44). Otherwise, ask them a few questions so that

you know some basic facts about their background. It is important to know how long they have been in the country, whether they have attended school here before, the length of time they have been learning English, and whether they have experienced interruptions in their formal education.

- Seat the students so that they have a good view of you and of the blackboard. Summarize important information on the board so that students whose English is limited have the opportunity to absorb key information visually as well as aurally. If students have to take home forms or attendance cards for a parental signature, make a short note on the board that states the date on which they must be returned. If you are introducing the students to your subject, write brief headings for topics as you deal with them. In Home Room, new students should be provided with a map of the school; the system for room numbering should be explained.

- Appoint a classmate as the new student's "buddy". If there are other students in the class who speaks that language, you may ask one of them to be the "buddy". This can be very helpful in facilitating exchanges of information in the first days of settlement. Conversely, there may be good reason to choose a student who does not speak the newcomer's native language. If the person chosen is responsible and kindly, s/he may be able to help the student to integrate better into the class as a whole. Students who speak the same language are likely to develop strong bonds and friendships, whether or not they are given responsibility for introducing the new class member to the procedures of the school.

- Give yourself and the class time on that first day to become acquainted with new students. If the group is your home room class, pair up the students and get them to interview each other. When finished, they may introduce each other to the rest of the class. Ask the students to limit themselves to three questions so that new students will not find the activity daunting. Play a game that requires everyone to remember everybody else's name. Join in yourself. It's amazing how frequently students do not know, or cannot remember, their teacher's name! In many cultures, teachers are addressed by a formal title to which no name is attached so this is an especially useful activity for your newcomers. One simple game is to have one student speak her name, the next to repeat the first student's name and to state his own, the third student to repeat the first two names and add hers, and so on, around the class.

- When reviewing the timetable with the class, make sure that new students are aware of others in the group who are going to the same classroom. State plainly that students who become confused or lost in the first few days can always return to the home room for help. If your school is large and students require equipment for certain classes, locks for their lockers, and so on, make sure that your students know where, when, and for how much they are able to obtain such articles.

A supportive climate in your classroom will encourage students to participate in the learning process and enable them to be successful in their efforts. The teacher is largely responsible for setting the tone in the classroom. Acknowledge the presence of students from different cultures. Encourage all students to share the richness of experiences available when working with people who have a wide variety of cultural backgrounds. During the course of the year, capitalize on opportunities to promote intercultural discussions, examine cultural similarities, and have differences explained. It is important to give students from other cultures opportunities to be the expert. You will find that in these circumstances, many students are more willing to speak, and can articulate thoughts and arguments much more freely. In general, when teachers establish a receptive, inquiring and respectful climate, in which all students feel their contributions to discussions and other classroom activities are valued, students are encouraged to take risks with language, to express their thoughts, and to be less self-conscious about speaking English.

Whatever subject you are teaching, allow your students who are learning English time to adjust. Encourage their participation, but don't put too much pressure on them initially. Although their receptive skills are probably much greater than they appear in the beginning, most students will be occupied with adjusting to your voice and the flow of class activities. Given this situation, you can still make clear your long-term expectations. Give an outline of the subject content and a list of required assignments. Let students know how their work will be evaluated. (Be sure that students are aware of the fact that they can receive extra help with their school work.) Students will feel more confident if they are given this information in written form so they can refer to it later, as well as reviewing it with you in class. A written introduction to the course might include a list of the objectives for the class, a description of the kinds of assignments that will be set, and a breakdown of the final mark that states the value of the term work, tests, and examinations.

Here are some longer-term strategies that will encourage students to feel self-confident and more inclined to participate fully in classwork and other school activities.

Strategies to Build Confidence

- Show a personal interest in your students and get to know them as individuals. Help students to feel they belong by greeting them when you meet them around the school and initiating conversations outside of class time. As you discover more about your students' experiences and ambitions, you will be more sensitive to their needs.
- Encourage students to attend school functions, and to join in school activities. Discuss sports that your students are interested in or play. Ask class members who belong to school clubs to describe the activities of those clubs. Encourage students to become involved in extracurric-

ular activities that you are responsible for supervising.

- Let students from the same cultural or linguistic background help one another. Support co-operative and coaching efforts by students whose English is strong. Cultural identity is closely tied to the use of students' native language. The psychological support of working with others of the same linguistic background and making use of their first language can prevent newcomers from feeling isolated and build their sense of self-worth. At the same time, remember to encourage the use of English. Make clear that your aim is to have all students understand the topic and be able to express their thoughts in English.

- To encourage participation, give students time to prepare oral answers whenever possible, perhaps by setting questions as homework, and then allowing students to read their answers in class. A tactic to use in class is to ask a student a question and to give time for the formulation of an answer by asking a second student to respond to another question. When s/he is finished, return to the original student who will have had time to compose a reply. Be patient and wait for a response if students are struggling; remember that these students are concerned about both the content and the form of their answer. If the teacher seems impatient, students may become nervous. The class, too, will lose interest.

- Show students how they can support their oral skills by using a variety of materials. Encourage them to use visual aids such as maps, charts, plans, graphs, and so on, when making oral presentations. Have students work in small groups to prepare projects so that they can more easily express opinions, and plan and develop arguments.

- When new students speak, concentrate on what they are trying to say, rather than on grammatical correctness. Avoid correcting oral contributions; instead give praise to answers that indicate effort, even if they contain errors.

- Give clear instructions and supplement oral directions with carefully-worded written instructions, especially about assignments. As an example, if students are to read a chapter in the textbook or an article for homework, discuss the topic in general terms ahead of time. Build a class glossary of key terms for the areas you are studying.

- Students will feel more confident if they are directed to supplementary materials in their own language, and to bilingual materials and dictionaries. Although it may not be possible to provide these in the classroom, the school library or resource centre can build such a collection. An early visit to the library to provide an introduction to such materials is therefore of great value.
- Encourage students' contribution and confidence by giving them a clear role in group work and class activities. (Remember to allow for adequate preparation time.) At first, students may contribute only visual aids to a group presentation and be reluctant to express their opinions in discussions. Wait a few weeks before asking these students to take a turn as the reporter for their group.

A combination of these strategies should help to create a supportive climate in the classroom, one in which all students feel comfortable and are able to put forth their best efforts. Recognizing each individual, encouraging them to show and build on their strengths, and fostering a cooperative spirit will give everyone the freedom to contribute to the joint learning of the group.

Out of the classroom, sharing information about the progress of students, asking for information about individuals from the ESL or Guidance departments, consulting students' school records, and gathering information about their previous education may all help in the design of flexible, sensitive, and relevant curriculum for all students.

In the classroom, observation will indicate how the students are progressing with the subject. Gestures, facial expressions, and other body language will give clues to how students are feeling and whether they are comfortable in the class. Observation provides the best means of getting to know students, their ambitions, skills, interests, and learning styles. It is only when we know our students that we can respond to their needs effectively.

SAMPLE INFORMATION FORM FOR CLASSROOM TEACHERS

To _____

From _____

Date _____

_____, a new student in the
ESL program has been enrolled in your _____
class in period _____. You may find the information below
helpful to you.

Approximate pronunciation of name (first) _____
(Last) _____
Country of origin _____
Location before Canada _____
Language(s) spoken _____
Length of time in Canada _____
Family members in Canada _____
Siblings in this school _____
Suggested translator _____ Home Form _____
Outside contact (English speaking) _____ Phone _____
Educational background _____
_____

Favorite subjects _____
Special skills and interests _____
Placement in ESL class _____ Period(s) ____ Teacher _____
Additional comments:

For further information please contact _____

CHAPTER 4

Assisting Students to Learn a Second Language

How We Learn a New Language

Many theories have been advanced on how best to teach a language; many more to explain how we learn our first language and how this may be applied to the learning of a second language. As a result, numerous methodologies that aim to promote language learning have been tested over the years. Some have been more successful than others, but in general, it has been shown that a combination of strategies has the best chance of success. This is partly because individual differences in the way people learn must be considered when teaching a large group. For some, the sounds of a new language may be easy to repeat — the intonations may give it a form, like music, that is easily remembered. For those people, learning to speak and understand a new language may be a swift process. For others, it may be a struggle; first, to separate the flow of unfamiliar sounds into meaningful units so that what is said can be understood, and secondly, to reproduce units of sound and meaning that may not exist within the person's first language.

Many people cannot accurately pronounce or remember words that they have not seen in written form. Given a text, however, they may be able to read and comprehend a large part of it. Since there is a great variety of writing systems in use in the world today, some students are still familiarizing themselves with the Roman alphabet and the sound symbol system during the first few months in their new

45

country. They may need simpler texts or extra help with reading, such as having the text read aloud and discussed in class, or exploring a text in a group, until their skills in reading and writing improve.

The function of a language is to give people the power to communicate thoughts, needs and feelings, to receive important information, to comprehend instructions, and to ask and answer questions. As students' become more proficient, their horizons widen; language for survival and everyday use has to be expanded to include a broader variety of vocabulary, structures, and grammar. Skills must be acquired so that they can absorb more complex information, read and research, make notes, organize and synthesize materials, think independently, express an opinion, and support it with well-developed arguments. All these skills are necessary for the intellectual growth of our students within their second language and their new society. In order to develop these skills, students must become fully engaged in the learning process and be willing to take risks. This requires an emotional commitment to learning the new language, in addition to an intellectual commitment. You can help students to take risks with language by giving praise to new or different ideas, encouraging everyone to express their opinions, and helping students to feel that their thoughts and feelings are valued.

For some, however, a second language has a practical rather than an emotional value for a long time. Such students may be less willing to take risks with the new language, and may need more encouragement to participate in the classroom. They may live in such a way that their social and emotional lives are conducted in their native language. The creation of a supportive and encouraging climate, which fosters friendly cooperation among all members of the class, will help these students to become a part of the group. As they form cross-cultural friendships, these students will find it easier to join in the give and take of the class.

The image of the student as a silent, passive learner is

one that has been rejected in recent years. When you see new students listening anxiously but saying very little, you may worry that they will not participate fully in the work planned for your class. You may also notice that they find oral participation especially difficult. The first written assignment may increase your anxiety; pre-discussion of the topic may not have guaranteed that all students have understood what was asked of them, and some may not have used conventional ways to express their ideas. Suddenly, your worries balloon. These students will never make it! It is easy (but far too hasty) to conclude that they shouldn't be in this class.

The students, however, may feel that they are beginning to 'get the hang of it'. In the first few days, they have become used to your voice and to the routines of the class, and are now struggling to comprehend and manipulate unfamiliar material. Slowly, the vocabulary, the texts, and the activities are becoming more meaningful. What is required is clearer. Although they may not be able to produce written work without errors, and may still be hesitant to express their thoughts orally, they are learning a great deal. Students' receptive skills are usually greater than their productive ones. Moreover, in the beginning, their anxiety or lack of confidence may affect how quickly they learn. Over the course of the year or semester, they will need plenty of opportunities to practise their speaking and writing skills. Students who are learning English need time to become accustomed to the core subject classroom.

In the ESL classroom, the program is designed to help the student develop listening, speaking, reading and writing skills in an interrelated way. Everyday life, personal experiences, our society (past and present), other cultures, current events, and social issues may provide some of the matter to be studied, and serve as the basis for discussion and written assignments. The course must be student-centred and flexible enough to address topics that are relevant to the particular group of students being taught. The content is important. We can't listen to, speak, read, or write about "nothing". It is through the study of specific topics that language is generated. In a core subject classroom, although students may need some assistance in developing their language skills, it is important to maintain the maximum amount of content possible.

Students need to study and learn in depth about subjects and topics that are of interest and importance to them. As they listen and read, they are acquiring knowledge, not only about the subject, but about how language works. As students solve problems, prepare answers, or take part in discussion, they are subconsciously using knowledge of the structure of the language to construct a medium of communication. Even though their speech and writing may contain approximations of expression, it is the creation of these communications that makes the language their own. Focusing on the topic allows them to become less self-conscious, and gives them the practice that will eventually allow them to become fluent.

A Strategy That Works: Co-operative Learning

Co-operative learning ensures that the individual's contribution is necessary to the completion of a particular task and to the learning process. Pair and group work should be organized so that students recognize the importance of their contribution. If group work is not carefully planned, the work may not be shared equally. This is not to say that all such work must have a formal structure, but ways must be found to monitor joint efforts so that students realize the value of their own work and are given credit for it.

Setting tasks that require students to use listening, speaking, reading, and writing skills should be an objective in all classes. Often, work in pairs and small groups can provide these opportunities. Co-operative learning also contributes to the students' sense of self-worth and builds their self-confidence.

Group work may be organized to achieve different goals. It may be used as a means to promote greater understanding of a difficult text, to solve problems, to synthesize a selection of different viewpoints, or to produce a major presentation or piece of written work. Informal pair or small group work may be made an ongoing part of normal class activity that does not require formal evaluation, but that does allow students to consult, discuss, and formulate answers co-operatively. Consequently, the work requires students to listen, speak, read, and write in order to complete an assignment. Teacher observations, anecdotal comments, and peer and self-evaluation checklists provide appropriate monitoring of such activities.

Groups may be asked to come up with questions on a story, essay, or piece of scientific text that the class has read. These questions can serve as the foundation of a whole class discussion or given to another group for their response. Problems of a mathematical, social, or ethical nature can be discussed by small groups and the results reported to the class. Large projects involving research, reporting, and the creation of a joint presentation also provide an opportunity for students to contribute to the learning of the class as a whole.

More elaborate methods of conducting group work, such as the "jigsaw", may have a place in your classroom. This method fosters the interdependency that is characteristic of co-operative learning. The "jigsaw" can facilitate the study of more difficult material that otherwise might remain incomprehensible to the individual. This method has students divide the information, examine different viewpoints separately, and build in time for the discussion of each section of the material. Co-operation is required of group members as they report on their segment and consolidate all the information given to the group. The group is then ready to answer a set of final questions and develop an opinion about the topic. When carefully constructed, the "jigsaw" can be an excellent introduction to the discussion of broad issues, such as pollution, industrialization, and conservation. Materials for the "jigsaw" can be culled from a wide variety of sources, and span a range of levels of difficulty so that multi-level groups can be formed to do the work together.

While our primary concern may be to engage students in active, integrated learning, there will be times when one language skill is of crucial importance. How can we help students to maximize those skills? Here are some suggestions:

Listening

- When you speak to the class as a whole, give students time to get used to your voice and manner. Make your instructions clear and brief.
- Avoid asking new students questions on their first day. Make your first question one that can be answered simply. If students are successful the first time, they will become more self-confident and will be encouraged to participate in the future.
- Ensure that students listen to each other by encouraging and acknowledging student contributions to class work. Give students opportunities, in pair and group work, to contribute information and ideas that are essential to joint efforts.
- Seat students where they can see both you and the blackboard clearly. Comprehension is enhanced when we can see the speaker's facial expression and interpret body language.
- If you are going to speak at length, give the students a brief outline of what you are going to say, or record an outline on the board as you speak. If you are explaining and elaborating on a chapter in a textbook, write the title and page reference on the board as you begin. Alternatively, have the students prepare for your lecture by reading the chapter as homework the night before.
- If you wish students to make notes from an oral presentation, give them a handout of headings and sub-headings. This can be a complex task for some students, requiring them to hear, understand, make quick judgements about

what is important, and write at speed. Notes taken in class and from textbooks should be checked periodically, and suggestions made so that note-taking skills can be improved over the course of the year. Students can be assisted in taking useful notes from reading matter if they are given a set of questions to answer. These help them to identify important information in the text.

- Visual aids, such as pictures, posters, maps, charts, diagrams, graphs, photographs, films, and video can be of tremendous assistance to new students. They increase comprehension of concepts, illustrate unfamiliar ideas, situations and backgrounds, and deepen understanding of the spoken or written word. As an example, general objects (e.g., photographs of the prairies and late nineteenth century farm life), and pictures of objects that have a symbolic or metaphorical value (e.g., peonies), help students to enter the world of Margaret Laurence's *The Stone Angel*.

Speaking

- Oral contributions are an important element in class participation, but for the student learning English, they may be the most problematic. Whenever possible, give students time to formulate oral answers and practise oral presentations with you and with other students. During class discussions, encourage participation by asking quieter students for their opinions on particular points. When asking a question, address it to a student by using his/her name. Wait a moment for the answer and discourage other students from prompting.
- Students communicate best when they feel confident about themselves and what they want to say. Encourage your students who are learning English to help others; explaining something they understand to a student who is having difficulty often provokes them to be more articulate. Similarly, seek opportunities to use those students as "experts" on certain topics. Their oral skills are

enhanced when they speak about something important to them and want to convey their thoughts and feelings.

- Make sure that all students know that oral participation is evaluated. Tell them how you plan to track it. In other cultures, where students pass or fail on the results of written examinations, oral participation may not be evaluated at all.
- Create a supportive climate in the classroom, in which all students' contributions are valued, and the exchange of ideas is a primary objective. When students speak, avoid making corrections; however, be ready to help out with vocabulary and the clarification of ideas.
- Design assignments and class work so that there is a real need to communicate orally. Work in pairs or small groups can facilitate this communication.

Reading

- Use a variety of pre-reading activities. For example, to prepare for study of a new topic, introduce the subject by discussing what the students already know. Make a glossary of key terms on the board, or prepare a handout. Some teachers have found it useful to compile a binder of difficult vocabulary as an ongoing project in the class. This provides all students with a permanent reference.
- Introduce the students to the textbooks they will use. Point out their strengths and weaknesses, tables of contents, headings, sub-headings, marginals, and indices. It may be useful to set a short assignment when students explore a textbook using these organizers;
- Use as many supplementary reading texts as possible. Suggest alternatives to the textbooks that can be obtained in the library or resource centre. A variety of reading materials, including newspapers, magazines, and peer and teacher writings may be useful. You may wish to abridge, adapt, or simplify the vocabulary used to describe a particular topic. Look for well-illustrated readings in magazines and books, and for concise, simply-written reference

works. Encyclopedias and dictionaries written for children and adolescents can be fruitful resources. Examples include *The Oxford Junior Encyclopedia* and *The Visual Dictionary*.

- Students are not always aware of what they are reading for. Give specific directions about the kind of reading they should be doing to complete their assignment: scanning the text for information, skimming to get the main idea, reading it slowly to absorb details, and so on.
- On occasion, reading aloud by the teacher may be helpful to the students so they can listen for rhythms, intonations, ironies, and other subtleties in the text. All students enjoy a dramatic reading of a passage. Students acquiring English language skills benefit from hearing something read while following the text with their eyes. Comprehension can also be enhanced by the use of videos, films, or audiotapes of the material being studied.

Writing

- Writing tasks should be varied, and should include personal writing and journal entries. Give students clear directions and plenty of practice in developing different kinds of writing. Some students may need to be shown how to write a report of a scientific experiment. Give them opportunities to do this, with a partner and on their own. Journals can provide opportunities for personal writing, or for an ongoing response to reading or to other work. You will be able to dialogue with your students by responding to their written ideas. A Health and Well-being journal, in which students record their activities and feelings, could be a project for a Physical Education class.
- Give guidance on note-taking — a series of questions can provide a good outline. Give instruction about summarizing, finding key words, and classifying and dividing notes;
- Follow all the steps of the writing process:
  pre-writing discussion — brainstorm and discuss ideas;
  writing first drafts;

conferencing with the teacher and other students — give help with grammar, structure, reorganization of ideas, coherence and unity;

revising and writing final drafts — encourage students to improve their work;

displaying and publishing student work.

Help students to follow these steps by giving them a checklist to fill in as they work through this process.

- Set assignments that grow out of class discussion or teacher explanations. A response to a reading or to a film gives students a meaningful context in which to express their ideas. Place emphasis on the process of writing and on content.
- If you want student writing to follow a particular form, make students aware of this and of how to write in this style. While going through the steps of the writing process, make sure that students receive responses to their writing, both from you and from other students. Students learn a great deal from each other. Read aloud and display examples of good student work. Praise and public acknowledgement of good effort will encourage students to continue writing.

Finally, in the teaching of any subject, bear in mind that all students have their own ways of learning. Vary your methods to accommodate different learning styles. By giving students a range of activities and reinforcing knowledge in a variety of interactive ways, you provide all students with a better chance of understanding and applying the content of the course.

CHAPTER 5

Program Planning and Adaptation

There is an overriding philosophical concern related to the process of learning that you must consider before you begin to plan or adapt a program for students who are acquiring English language skills. This concern focuses on the question of the extent to which the content of the curriculum takes precedence over the processes that students are engaged in as they experience learning. While curriculum content is certainly of great importance, many recent studies carried out in a number of countries indicate that the most effective learning takes place when students are actively participating in their own learning.

What does this mean for you as curriculum planner? It means that for any program that you plan to teach, the prime objective is to make possible, and promote, students' playing an active role in their own learning. Obviously, this has major implications for methodologies and strategies that you might plan to use. Therefore, expect that most of your creative energy will be focused on this aspect of program development. In order to do this, you may have to free yourself and your program from some of the demands of curriculum content. You may even find yourself committing the "heresy" of unloading some of the content. Once you have accepted this, you may find the freedom intellectually and pedagogically refreshing. Otherwise, the danger arising from a content-based curriculum is that you will focus your energies, and those of your students', on the acquisition of large amounts of content for its own sake. Inevitably, this tyranny of curriculum content comes at the expense of opportunities students would otherwise be given to acquire concepts, skills, attitudes, and problem-solving strategies — the mark of true learning. In addition, an emphasis on the teaching of content does not often allow time for you to tailor parts of your program to meet the local needs of your students in specific areas, or for the integration of topics of study across the curriculum, where concepts may be reinforced in a variety of ways in different subject classes.

Collaborative Curriculum Planning

Authorization of teachers to take initiatives in planning curriculum requires the trust and support of administrators. As an individual teacher acting as researcher in your classroom, you can gain excellent insights through the use of untried strategies to change and improve curriculum. Mentoring and peer coaching arrangements, joint development of curriculum, and greater communication and collaboration between core subject departments and ESL departments is to be encouraged. Your mutual exchange of strategies for developing language skills in formal and informal ways, and helpful suggestions for preparing students for subject classes will be beneficial to teachers and students alike. The establishment of interdepartmental links to develop curriculum will help you to focus on making connections between students' previous and present education, between their experiences in different subject classes, and between concepts and concrete examples. Their learning experience will be more relevant and the curriculum less fragmented.

Planning time must be scheduled if commitment to program change is to develop. In secondary schools, subjects have traditionally been segregated into specific departments. Through collaboration, many issues can be effectively addressed across several areas of the curriculum. To this end, consider inviting curriculum consultants to assist your departments in developing curricula and to ensure that they meet system and Ministry expectations.

You will be challenged to achieve a balance between what must be taught and a varied repertoire of methodologies that develop language and enhance thinking skills. Meet with your department to select certain areas of content as fundamental. Discuss *how* they should be taught; other areas may be designated as less important so individual teachers can have some discretion in their treatment of them. When you collaborate across the curriculum and share responsibility for curriculum development, you make your subject more relevant by connecting it to the wider experience of the students. This will enhance the learning outcomes for all students. In addition, developing in students the capacity to co-operate, think for themselves, and draw on their total experience to adapt to a rapidly changing future must form part of the goals of any successful curriculum.

Using Students' Experiences to Create Curriculum

When planning curriculum, it is important to draw on the varied backgrounds, cultural traditions, and life experiences of your students to create curriculum, and to develop in students feelings of pride, tolerance, and mutual respect. By doing this, you provide students with opportunities to share their expertise, build self-esteem, and increase cross-cultural understanding for all of your students. As examples:

- In a Physical Education class, introduce a sport familiar to your new students, such as soccer, cricket, or table tennis. They will be the experts who can teach the rules and strategies of these sports to the other students.
- In the case of a subject such as Mathematics, a strategy could be built around independent study projects, an important component of the learning process in all subject curricula. A Mathematics project could look at such topics as past and present number systems, international

strategy games, and alternative strategies students have previously learned in solving Mathematics problems.

- In a History program, a meaningful unit of study for your students could be past and present immigration experiences, and their impact on the receiving countries. A multicultural unit or independent study projects focusing on the history of various cultural groups would also motivate your students and give them a feeling of pride.
- In Science, you might ask your students to research inventions by people from other cultures.

Taking Down the Walls

Collaboration between teachers in several subject areas to produce a cross-curricular unit of study with a multicultural focus has great potential. The History, Geography and English departments could explore the immigrant experience from different perspectives. In the History component, the social and economic aspects of immigration could be explored. In Geography, students would be learning about patterns of immigration, demographics, the changing face of cities, land use, and the ways in which geography has affected the settlement of immigrants. In English classes, students could be developing communication skills by preparing reports for presentation in the History and Geography classrooms. Students could also engage in role-playing activities and dramatizations of immigrant experiences, based on personal experiences and on the reading of selected literature dealing with the theme of the immigrant experience. As a result of participating in such a project, the students will realize that they are not so different; their experiences have been shared by innumerable people in different parts of the world through the centuries.

When choosing materials to support the curriculum, give attention to those that reflect the multicultural composition of the student body. Infusing the curriculum with first language and bilingual materials enhances students' self-concept when they realize that their first language is recognized and valued. Such materials are valuable additions to school and classroom libraries. Research has shown that growth in second language acquisition is positively affected by maintenance of the learner's first language.

Education for Social Justice

In the teaching of all subject areas, it is important to motivate your students by bringing in the real world as they know it. A relevant and meaningful curriculum is vital for piquing the interest of all students. An added bonus of such a curriculum is the fostering of mutual respect and understanding that will help to build a more tolerant society. Caution must be exercised in the selection of course texts and classroom collections. These books must be examined critically to ensure that they include information about the history and traditions of various cultures and promote intercultural understanding. Provide opportunities for your students to discuss, debate, detect bias and prejudice, and form judgments about issues that affect the lives of minorities living in their local community and throughout the world. Such activities will increase your students' self-esteem, build respect for others, and develop their critical thinking skills.

Anxiety Attacks/Curriculum Angst

You will probably hear concerns expressed by some of your colleagues about the legitimacy of the credits they are granting in their subject areas. As well, they will question whether students are adequately prepared for college or university, given that their high-school courses have been modified to suit their language abilities. To ease your colleagues' concern, hold preliminary meetings with all departments to discuss course goals. As a group, decide which topics across the breadth of the curriculum are crucial for students' progress in subsequent years; the validity of your program will then become more evident. You may need to become more experimental in your teaching and to take some risks. Each new group of students is different, and has different needs. As you gain experience with each group of students, revision of strategies will be necessary. Collaboration among colleagues who feel free to discuss their failures along with their successes, will contribute to collective expertise in planning and delivering curriculum.

Language Across the Curriculum

When planning programs for the various areas of the curriculum, each subject department should give attention to how the language skills of listening, speaking, reading, and writing can be developed through the teaching of content. For some activities, particularly in academic courses, you may want to emphasize reading and writing skills. In other courses, aural/oral skills may receive more attention. Wherever possible, however, all skills should be integrated so that language skills are developed holistically in meaningful contexts.

It is sometimes thought that the second-language learner must have particular difficulties in understanding concepts, abstractions, and generalities. Perhaps this is because we assume that the meaning of the concept lies in the words we use to describe it. This is not strictly true. A concept can be described in many different words and in many different languages. Understanding concepts and abstractions is something that many adolescents find difficult in their own language. We often try to help young people grasp concepts by dealing with concrete examples first, and then by pointing out the connections between them. On other occasions, we present students with an abstract idea and ask them to relate this to their own experience. Drawing on previous experience and knowledge, students are often expected to make a leap of understanding, to generate new knowledge and greater comprehension for themselves. The key to this process is the ability to make connections and to weave our experiences and fragmented knowledge into a web. As an example, many immigrant students have had firsthand experience of war, extreme poverty, homelessness or tyranny — dangers that most school students have never had to face. While such matters need to be treated carefully, these students will have a deeper understanding of these concepts and can be encouraged to contribute their perceptions to the class. In helping students to make connections with their previous experience, you may need to take a fresh look at the material you want to use in class. To take a specific example, if you are reading Wilfred Owen's sonnet, "Anthem to Doomed Youth", have students discuss funerary rituals practised in different cultures before examining the contrasts between the recognition given to the death of those who die in peace and those who are killed in wars. This will encourage a better understanding of the theme, as well as the structure of the poem.

Students who are learning English need assistance in developing the vocabulary to draw on what they already know, and the reassurance that what they know is valid. These students need opportunities to explore the connections between what they have learned and what they are learning. If given assistance, they are as capable of grasping a concept as an English-speaking student. Such assistance can be helpful to all the students in the class. As an example, in Science it is frequently the case that the class is unfamiliar with the scientific terms relating to a specific topic. Exploring the language, as well as the topic, is productive for the class as a whole. By developing definitions as a group, compiling a glossary of scientific terms or discussing related words you will be contributing to a greater understanding of the language of Science by all students.

Technology and scientific principles are studied and applied world-wide. With encouragement, students can make connections between the world outside as they have experienced it and what goes on in the classroom. Moreover, since Science classes demand a hands-on, experiential approach to the material, students are able to engage in activities that are non-linguistic in nature, but are necessary to the learning process and to comprehension. Consider too, that concepts can be contextualized in the classroom and that the study of Science offers many opportunities for this. As students absorb knowledge of the subject and increase their understanding of fundamental concepts, they also learn and use language in a meaningful context. In a Science class, students will learn how to take linear and liquid measurements. The concept of measurement will be familiar to all students in their own language, and they can draw upon this understanding by actively participating in experiments with different kinds of measuring tools.

Similarly, in other classes, it is essential to call upon your students' understanding of concepts, generalizations, abstractions, and culture-based experience to illuminate the study of topics in the classroom. Students may bring different viewpoints to the discussion of economics, politics, world issues, or literature that can extend and deepen the class experience. In History, Geography, Social Sciences and English, cross-cultural references, multicultural examples and materials, and opportunities for your students to share their experiences encourage second-language learners to approach tasks as whole persons, fully engaged in the learning process.

Modifying a Science Lesson

In a Science class, you may find yourself in a situation where special materials to support your program may not be readily available. As a result, you will probably use the same textbook as is used by mainstream classes. How can you adapt material from the text, make it accessible to students, and not lessen its value and content? The strategies that follow can help you with this task. By employing these strategies, you make the study of Science a vehicle for language acquisition. As well, you introduce students to the scientific method, and help them to question, understand, and appreciate the world they live in. Similar strategies can be applied to modify curriculum in other subject areas.

Strategies

- Words inherent in the study of science are important vocabulary items for your students to understand. Adapt definitions by giving them alternative words that they may be more familiar with. Take some time to discuss the meaning of suffixes in words such as *colorless* and *odorless*.
- Explain that *purpose* means "why we are doing the experiment"; *materials* are "what we are using to do the experiment"; *caution* means "be careful"; *procedure* means "what we do in the experiment"; *discussion* means "what you talk about", and so on.
- Through your demonstrations, your students can observe experimental techniques and, through guessing, hypothesizing, predicting, inferring and questioning, reach conclusions about specific problems. Provide hands-on opportunities for students to work in pairs or small groups to practise scientific methods by investigating, discussing, recording, and analyzing data. Let them feel and handle a variety of items to help you convey the meaning of nouns and adjectives.
- Have a dictionary of science, a picture dictionary, or other pictorial materials available in your classroom. When words fail, pictures can often convey meaning instantly. Your library resource teacher or curriculum consultant may be able to help you find materials to support your topic. With your students, develop your own classroom glossary of terms that you can add to as the course progresses.
- Do some initial examples with your students. By observing you, they will have a clearer idea of how to proceed. Use an overhead projector to show students how to fill in scientific charts.

- Break down assignments into manageable bits. Ask students to do a small portion of a task (e.g., describing five substances used in an experiment). Take up the answers before asking the students to continue with the rest of the assignment. In this way, misunderstandings can be cleared up before proceeding with the remainder of the assignment.
- Have the students work in pairs or small groups where they can discuss the answers to questions. This will help them to clarify their understanding before they attempt to write their answers.
- Be sure that your students understand homework instructions. Explain clearly what you are asking them to do.

CHAPTER 6

Evaluating Students

In recent years, changing educational philosophy has resulted in many innovations in classroom practice. The emphasis on student-centred learning and the whole-language approach to education are two such examples. The need to facilitate transitions made by students from one school to another, and from one culture to another has encouraged a re-examination of what we do in the secondary school years. Suggestions for greater integration of curriculum that will address the needs of individuals in a holistic manner are changing our ideas about the nature of curriculum. Contemporary teaching practices that support an interactive, holistic approach to learning have led the way to changes in methods of evaluation.

Observation is the Key

Evaluation by observation has led to less emphasis on tests and examinations, even in senior grades. This has meant that more attention can be given to the learning process, and to the work done on an everyday basis. Teachers have developed new evaluative techniques to record process and progress. As well, these methods take into consideration a wider variety of activities such as: the assessment of higher thinking skills as demonstrated by students' abilities to solve problems; students' ability to apply what they have learned to new situations; and their ability to communicate their ideas in a variety of ways. Opportunities to videotape students in the process of approaching and dealing with a problem now provide greater insight into the whole range of performance demonstrated by students at any particular level. Over time, these examples can be gathered and developed into a reference library. Samples of student writing can be collected and analyzed by groups of teachers to establish criteria for holistic evaluation. Such conferences may well lead to innovative approaches to program delivery. Keeping a record of your anecdotal comments made on a weekly basis, or keeping student checklists on aspects of the learning process that are important to success in your subject will help you monitor students' progress. Students should keep a writing folder containing all their writing. If all pieces are dated, they can easily see how much their writing has improved over the year.

Are these innovations of benefit to the students? Ongoing, continuous assessment, and observation of the students' performances in a variety of contexts over a period of time give you and your students the opportunity to monitor progress. You will be able to identify areas in which students need help, and aspects of the curriculum that need further attention. Peer evaluation is especially helpful to students. As students discover how they can help one another, they become better able to evaluate their own performance, a first and crucial step in improving their work.

Evaluation serves a double purpose in that it provides information both for students and teachers. Assist your students in self-assessment efforts so that they may become aware of their strengths and weaknesses and be encouraged to continue their efforts. Assess the program's success. Adapt content, strategies, and materials to improve its effectiveness. Monitoring progress informs both teacher and students about individual achievement, and that of the class. At various points in the year, assessment of general achievement by means of major assignments, tests, or examinations is necessary. Prepare your students for these. The format and design of the assessment tools, as well as their language, should allow the students opportunities to display their strengths and knowledge. Make sure your students have had practice in answering the types of questions that will appear on the examination or test.

How to Evaluate

What should we be looking at when assessing students' abilities in the classroom setting? A variety of skills can be evaluated by observation. Provide feedback to students on how they perform individually and as part of a group engaged in co-operative efforts. Participation, effort, attitude and enthusiasm, progress in daily work, projects, assignments, and presentations should all be monitored and reported on, either in interviews or in written form (sometimes in both). This kind of evaluation is an integral part of the teaching-learning process. Since some learners are at first shy in class, informal interviews to discuss their progress can encourage them to participate more fully. As students relax and adjust to the classroom, you will be able to observe how they handle tasks, and how they transfer knowledge and skills to a new situation and work independently.

Implications for Designing Assignments and Courses

Assignments that demand a combination of skills to reach a real outcome or that offer students the opportunity to solve a problem will give you a better insight into students' performance and progress. These assignments may be designed for individual or group attention. In either case, intervene and prompt students when they need your help — this will encourage more sophisticated work and increase comprehension. If interaction is maintained at a supportive level, students will become more confident. It may be that students learning English will have some difficulties in composing a finished, written "product" as the conclusion to a complex project. Assessment, however, can take into consideration the organization and preparations that preceded the final product. Some methods students might find less threatening include using taped interviews or presenting their final reports and presentations in the form of a poster display. Encouraging variety will allow students to develop their own special talents. By taking part in group projects, or by doing assignments individually, students can develop the skills they need to become more fully engaged in their own learning.

- In assessing students' comprehension of a topic, give students alternative ways of showing that they have understood a concept (e.g., those with weak verbal skills can use illustrations and charts). Role-playing, formulating questions, oral presentations, and debates are all means for assessment, as well as ways to promote learning. An assortment of assignments will give students a better chance to exercise a variety of skills and to demonstrate their strengths.
- Some kinds of assessment are particularly stressful for new students. Tests and examinations can be made fairer for these students by allowing the use of a dictionary, by wording questions in a concise manner, perhaps by breaking down complex questions into a series of smaller questions, and by allowing students extra time to complete the work. Some students will be unfamiliar with the kinds of questions used in tests: practice is needed in answering multiple-choice questions, short answers, essays, or any other kind of question you plan to use on your tests.
- Students may also find oral assessment threatening, despite a fair degree of fluency. Increase students' confidence by giving them time to rehearse their presentation with you and with other students. At this time, they can be encouraged to improve audibility and pronunciation.
- Decide on the criteria for evaluation before the course begins, preferably collegially as a department or with other teachers of the course. As well, make students aware of how they are to be evaluated at the outset of the course. Language and content are closely linked, but if students can convey ideas clearly enough to be under-

stood, students should receive credit for the content. Should a student still experience difficulties at the end of the year or semester, it is preferable to give a NMA (No Mark Assigned) designation rather than to report the low marks earned. The assignment of low marks will discourage the student who may need a longer period to adjust and improve. On the other hand, students understand and approve of standards in teaching and learning. If, at the end of the year, they have not managed to pass, they will have laid a good foundation for repeating the course the following year, should they wish to. This is particularly true in the case of those who have joined the class part way through the year; the class will have given them the opportunity to make themselves at home and to prepare themselves for future progress.

- To encourage success, make sure that your students know what your expectations are. Sometimes it is helpful to give students a written guideline detailing your expectations for all the students in your class. This can include expectations for class behavior, completion of homework, the preparation of assignments, information about how to catch up with work after an absence, and how to get extra help. You can also help students improve their work by giving them written instructions and helpful tips on how to do complex tasks, such as writing an essay. Many students may need guidance in the development of proper study habits since a subject may initially seem overwhelming. The teaching of study skills will be of benefit to all your students.

Teaching and curriculum for the whole child, adolescent, or adult naturally leads to the use of a wider variety of evaluative techniques and encourages more flexible programming.

Everyday activities which can be assessed might include:

- responses to viewing
- discussion, analyzing, synthesizing, generalizing
- role-playing, dramatizing

- experimenting, hypothesizing, predicting, investigating
- reporting orally or in writing
- skimming and scanning for information
- making notes
- preparing and giving a talk
- creating questions to indicate understanding or to find out more
- creating a picture or sketch in response to reading
- writing in a variety of modes — letters, writing in role, journals, reports, short answers, compositions, essays, and so on.

A student writes. . .

Starting new life in a country with new standards and expectations was the kind of experience that I shall never be able to forget.

I arrived in Canada in mid october 1987. At the beginning, because of my lack of knowlege of the language and the calture every thing and every body seemed shinny and nice, but as the time passed by I started to anderestand and see the more realistic face of the new society, which was craul and selfish. Then I realized that in order to survive in such society, I had to try to become one of them, in other word I had to blend in, ina way that I could not be recogenized as a forigner, since a forimer was a bad news every where.

So in the proces of be comming westernized I started to lose my Identiti, up to the point that I had difficulty realizing who I was. Then I tested the bitterness of emptyness. Somhow couiping with one problem had created another one. . As a result I lost the porpose of my eaistance and meaningless scence of self being.

In conclosion I should add that in the road of recovery I'm still no where.

CHAPTER 7

Responding to Issues

The Challenge for the Teacher

Adjusting to the influx of immigrant, refugee, and visa students may challenge teachers whose classes already contain students who have a wide variety of strengths and weaknesses. All students benefit, however, from analysis of their specific needs, and the provision of concrete learning materials, visual aids, and supplementary and enrichment texts. Draw on students' experiences. These can enrich your class. Contribute to your students' increased self-confidence and academic proficiency by giving them opportunities for active involvement in groups. These opportunities will enhance the advancement of capable learners and increase the gains made by second language learners. Such interaction among peers promotes positive academic friendships, and is a powerful motivator of achievement.

Students Speak Out

After students have been in the school system for a period of time and have had the opportunity to participate in multicultural leadership experiences, they are better able to voice the concerns of newcomers. It is important that these students' comments and thoughts are noted, since they have first-hand experience with the issues. Their suggestions can help schools to create a warm, welcoming environment in which students feel they are full participants in the educational experience.

Parents as Partners

Since parents are partners in the education of their children, parents' meetings merit careful planning. Finding interpreters who speak the various languages can be a challenge, however, increased contact between parents and the school encourages parental involvement in their children's education. Parents' understanding of what happens at school is increased when they can observe their children in class, or when they can participate with their children in a learning event, for example, conducting a science experiment. Topics for a parents' meeting agenda could include: explaining the credit system, the school timetable, the homework policy, how students will be evaluated, attendance procedures, how to get in touch with the school, who to talk to about specific problems, how to obtain the services of an interpreter, and so on.

The following concerns and corresponding suggestions have been commonly voiced by teachers, students, and parents.

Issues Raised by Teachers

Are students misplaced if they don't seem to have the background for the course in which they are placed? Should they be transferred to another class when this becomes apparent?

- Give students time to adjust. All placements should be regarded as tentative. Don't consider transferring students until you have had a one-on-one conference and have reviewed some of the work with them.
- Specific gaps may need to be filled, but students' placement in the course will have taken into consideration their potential and ability to learn.

72

How can we help students who don't seem to understand instructions, and are not able to read the textbook and understand technical terminology? Likewise, how can we help students who know the content and concepts but can't express them?

- Spend some time with those students who don't seem to be responding. A one-on-one talk will give you better information about the students' progress. Encourage those who are having difficulty to stay after class on certain days for extra help.
- Provide students with a variety of partners, some who speak the same language and others who speak English. There is a danger of "ghettoizing" students if they usually work in same-language groups. It is important to work toward cross-cultural partnerships.
- Give students tasks they can accomplish so that they are viewed as capable members of the class.

How can we do what is best for mainstream students when they are reluctant to work in groups with students who are learning English?

- The teacher has a role in setting the tone so that students feel accepted. Make clear the strengths of individuals and the contribution that everyone can make to the class.
- Develop co-operative skills by promoting friendly relations in the class. Encourage students to help one another. Give them opportunities to work together to improve individual work and produce group projects.
- Strategies commonly used to teach ESL students are usually worthwhile for all students. Make clear to the class that your objective is for everyone to learn the material required to pass the course. Students can be given responsibilities that require different levels of ability so that the joint task is accessible to all. Organize activities so that the maximum amount of English is spoken and facilitate the most tentative attempts to use language. Carefully planned group work can do this.
- Be prepared to encourage enrichment activities for all students in mixed ability groupings.

At the secondary school level, especially in the senior grades, we have guidelines to follow and a great deal of content to teach. Students have to meet certain standards and expectations. How can they do this if their English is not strong enough?

- Students may well be able to learn the content, as many have acquired excellent memorization skills. But it is the meaning behind the content that must be made clearer. Strategies that require students to apply what they are learning to new tasks and real-life situations will help them to make connections and will teach students some English as they are learning the content.
- In senior classes, give students support in learning the forms in which to give answers for your particular subject. Don't take for granted that they know the design and format expected for assignments. Knowing how to formulate answers helps students generate the right language for the task.
- Philosophical decisions to relinquish some content in order to teach learning skills may be necessary. Flexibility in planning curriculum content, in making cross-curricular connections, and in evaluative procedures must be sanctioned at the outset. It is possible to meet the needs of all students in the class, as well as the needs of the subject. Methodology appropriate for ESL learning, such as helping students to understand difficult subject textbooks or clarifying instructions, is equally appropriate for mainstream students.

We recognize that process, as well as product, is important, but the product must still be evaluated. How much can we change our methods of evaluation and still grant a legitimate credit?

- Formal, written work is not the only way to verify whether learning has occurred. Evaluation of the process forms an important part of overall evaluation. Understanding of concepts, clear thinking, and communication of essential ideas and information normally takes precedence over grammatical accuracy. Collaboration within departments, between schools, and with the Ministry of Education should be sought to gain approval for the flexibility needed for students to be evaluated fairly.

- A learning process is set up to produce a worthwhile product. If the process is carefully monitored, the product should be satisfactory. Part of the evaluative procedure should include assessment of the various steps followed during completion of the assignment.
- In mainstream classes, a small proportion of marks is deducted for grammatical structure, spelling, and syntax. Marking schemes should acknowledge both content and style, thereby allowing students to receive a legitimate credit in a subject. Conversely, if the work is incomprehensible after all the steps of the learning process have been followed, the student will be unsuccessful in the course.

What strategies are helpful in dealing with a transitory student population?

- Students are placed according to their ability and the time of year they enter the school. Teachers should assume students have some background in the subject area if they are placed in their classes part way through the school year.
- Late placements within the school year should be viewed as settlement placements, where students get used to their new school and learn some of the expectations of the subject area. Should they have insufficient background for the subject, they will have the opportunity to repeat it.
- New students may change the class dynamics. Finding a "buddy" for them and giving individual time and attention is important. Make contact with their ESL teacher to share insights on their progress.
- Within a system, students should be able to move from one school to another and study similarly-designed courses. Many students, however, are willing to travel a long distance in order to stay in the same class.

Issues Raised by Students

How can we make friends with Canadian students and improve students' and teachers' understanding of different cultural groups?

- A welcoming committee of students and staff might be organized to greet newcomers and help them in their early adjustment to school life.
- Schools can help to build friendships and encourage a sense of belonging by arranging for cross-cultural "buddies" for the students.
- Draw on the educational background, talents, and experiences of students from other countries. Make them valued resources in the curriculum. Encourage native-born students to use students from other cultures as resources when researching projects. Include the study of literature from other cultures or world Geography or History to improve intercultural understanding.
- Field trips that include newcomers and native-born students, accompanied by both mainstream and ESL teachers, encourage interaction outside the classroom setting.
- Encourage students to participate in extra-curricular activities, particularly in those in which their teachers are involved. This adds to their feeling of security, and teachers will get to know their students in a different setting.
- Cross-cultural understanding can occur through the formation of multicultural clubs, or by planning multicultural assemblies where Canadian traditions are celebrated along with those of other cultures. The friendships, co-operation, and mutual respect fostered by such events have lasting effects.
- Encourage ethnic groups to create displays about their culture for school bulletin boards or open house days. Validation of their traditions builds pride.
- An ESL newsletter or column in the school newspaper

can encourage the contribution of all students, and allow issues to be raised.

How can extra tutorial help, more counselling time, specific information about the school system, and more choice of options be made available?

- The guidance department might consider offering group guidance sessions at lunch time, when interested students could receive information about the educational system and the career paths available to them. Students often have difficulty with subjects for which they already have qualifications and may need to discuss alternative career aspirations. Allowing them to state their needs and voice their concerns may well lead to some program changes.
- Individual counselling sessions should be available to those students with personal or family problems. Students should be aware that they can have the help of an interpreter to explain their problems.
- More multilingual student support staff are always needed and could be of great assistance, especially to the more recently-arrived groups of students.
- Greater co-ordination of education, health, and social services would help the transition of students and their families into the new culture.

How can we become Canadian without losing our own culture?

- Students lead different lives in school and at home. This often causes tension between home and school. Students may adopt Canadian ways at school, and live at home within their own culture. They may want to participate in after-school activities or attend school dances, but face resistance from home. Teachers can sometimes help by speaking personally to parents about the importance of extra-curricular participation for a well-rounded school experience.
- Research has indicated that instruction in the students' native language contributes to their advancement in a new

77

language. Consider offering heritage classes, open to all students, to develop understanding of both the language and culture of other groups.

- Involve parents in the school by planning multicultural activities. Invite them to share their experiences and expertise with classes. Encourage them to volunteer their services for tutorial programs. This will help validate the students' home culture, and make parents more familiar with the culture of the school.

How can we be helped to learn the school rules? How can athletic facilities be more accessible and how do we sign up for activities and learn rules for games?

- Keep school rules to the minimum. Have assemblies at the beginning of the school year or semester to explain the rules to everyone. Review school rules periodically throughout the year in ESL classes as new students arrive.
- Have students develop their own handbook for newcomers or publish a newsletter containing articles about current sports, their rules, and how to sign up for teams.
- Encourage student participation in extra-curricular activities. Students will likely take a more active role when one of their teachers accompanies them or is the staff advisor or coach.
- Home form teachers or staff who sponsor athletic activities should take time to explain how students can sign up. Physical Education departments might consider having the rules for various sports translated into different languages.
- Consider establishing more team sports for beginners.

Issues Raised by Parents and the Community

What orientation and welcoming procedures are available to parents in the schools? We want to feel comfortable in the school environment and better understand the school culture, its programs, routines, policies, and expectations of our role.

78

- During the reception and welcoming procedures, parents should receive information regarding alternative school programs, options, and the credit system.
- Many schools have developed handbooks of information in various languages for students and their parents. Some have produced a videotape of school activities and procedures, with commentary in a variety of languages.
- Newsletters to parents can be translated into various languages, using the services of Board translators. Arranging for interpreters to telephone to the home is often helpful.
- The school can facilitate networking between parents who speak the same language and who can provide support, translation, and information to newcomers.
- Students can be encouraged to take home books in their first language, as well as in English. Some work in Science or Mathematics can be designed to be taken home and completed with the help of family members. This will broaden understanding of work done in school, encourage parent-child interaction, and may contribute to the literacy skills and educational development of family members.
- Teachers are encouraged to call the students' homes or write letters about specific school activities that require students to remain at school after dismissal time.

How do we get easier access to interpreters to assist in contacts with the school? How do we find out about the kinds of social services available to the community?

- Interpreters, social workers, psychologists, and school community advisors are employed by most Boards and may be contacted through the local school. There may be a delay in accessing their services because of their heavy workload. In emergencies, however, assistance can usually be found quickly.
- Cultural organizations may be of help to families if they require the services of an interpreter. Schools could provide a list of these organizations.

- A lot of information is availble free of charge to new-comers and can be given out at reception centres or in local schools. Manuals published by government and cultural organizations are available in many languages.

Are there ESL classes and classes in basic literacy for parents during the day and in the evening? Are child-care arrangements made available for parents who are attending classes, interviews, or parents' meetings?

- Some schools have established daycare facilities so that parents can learn English while their children are cared for by professional staff. Parents can also improve their English by taking young children to a parenting centre that provides opportunities for children to play together while parents socialize with one another.
- If necessary, parents should be encouraged to feel that they can bring young children to interviews. However, schools might consider organizing a group of students to provide babysitting services during parents' night.
- Some schools have had large turnouts at parents' meetings because they have arranged them at unusual times, for example, on a Sunday afternoon, so that parents who work at night can attend.

How can we be sure about our children's safety and security at school and while travelling to and from school?

- Our schools may seem very different from schools that children attended previously. Discipline may seem lax, both to students and their parents. Explanation of the school's code of behavior is important.
- Parents need to understand that the school's primary concern is to provide a safe learning environment for students, and that all schools have policies to deal with racial incidents, bullying, violence, and intruders in the school.
- Schools have rules that encourage all students and staff to treat one another with respect. If students or parents are involved in incidents with someone who defies the

rules, these perpetrators should be reported to teachers or administrators at the local school, to the Board, or to human rights organizations.

- One aim of education is to produce self-motivated, responsible citizens. Parents can encourage their children's self-confidence and independence by teaching them how to travel safely on their own. When possible, however, students should be encouraged to travel to and from school with friends who live nearby.

A student writes. . .

"Escape from my country"

About one o'clock in the morning my mother woke me up and told me to escape. I wore poor clothes at that time because my parents didn't want the government to know that I was escaping. When I stood in front of my house I turned back to my parents but I didn't say any thing because my eyes were filled with tears. I couldn't talk and I felt sad for them. I saw them cry and my younger sister, too. I went out to the bus station and waited for a minute for the bus to come and I got on to it. I looked at my house for the last time.

About four o'clock, my bus arrived at Can Tho and I transferred to another bus. At nine a.m. I arrived and waited at the bus station for somebody to come and guide me to their house. They put me in their room and I waited about 14 hours. When the sky grew dark, we started to go. It was not easy, I walked about 1 mile in the mud towards the sea. After that we got into a canoe and went around to find a big boat. The next day, we found a boat but we still waited a few hours because the steersman said he would find more canoes and people. When we had enough people, our boat started to go.

After three days, we didn't see land, only ocean around us. We didn't have enough food and water and we thought that maybe the next day we would die.

In the meantime, the waves were high and low. We didn't know if our boat would turn upside down. We thought maybe we would die. In the afternoon, we saw a big oil company's ship. They saved our lives and we were lucky. They brought us to the refugee camp.

This is only half the story. I can't tell more because everybody doesn't understand, and my English is not good enough to explain how I lived in the refugee camp, how the army behaved with the refugees. We had more happen and the fishermen killed a lot of people in the sea. They raped women and girls many times at once. I will never forget about our escape and crossing the ocean.

CHAPTER 8

Building Commitment

Invariably, planned and unplanned changes come about in schools. It is natural that the needs of a changing student body form the basis for planned school improvement. Responding to the situation entails reflecting on what your school is doing to help students adjust and what changes are necessary in order to facilitate this adjustment. How will you implement changes and what support or resources will you need to do this? What are the implications of these changes for your students? Discussion of some of these issues with your colleagues will help shape a vision for the school in the future.

Sharing Ownership

Schools develop an individual character through school-based decision-making and planning. In conjunction with your colleagues, take a role in developing a coherent plan for your school's improvement. Individual teachers often feel powerless to effect changes in policy, although they are willing to adopt innovations. By putting forward proposals and discussing changes with others, teachers can show their commitment to the school and to educational improvement. Administrators need to reassure staff that changes in curriculum and teaching strategies are not only sanctioned but encouraged. Some of your colleagues may need guidance in adapting their strategies to the changing student body.

Others may feel some regret that they can no longer teach in the way they did before. If all teachers express both positive ideas and negative feelings and share some of the responsibility for change, administrators can get everybody working together in the improvement process.

Your school staff can begin by. . .

Developing a Language Policy for the Whole School

Work collaboratively to develop a philosophical statement about the broad educational experience desired for all students in your school. In response to an increase in the number of students who require second language support, consider that:

- all teachers share responsibility for the teaching of language, since language is the vehicle for all learning;
- a supportive language environment will be created by adding language-oriented activities to the mainstream classroom;
- language support will need to be provided through appropriate ESL programming;
- staff should plan appropriate reception, welcoming, and orientation procedures in the school;
- all departments should make suggestions about how students are assessed and placed;
- with regard to second language learning, the role of the guidance department, student support services, curriculum departments, and individual teachers should be delineated;
- strategies for effective language teaching and evaluation should be shared across the curriculum.

Drawing Up a School-based Needs Assessment

Purpose

- to become acquainted with the cultural and linguistic composition of the school community;

- to develop an understanding on the part of all school staff of the system expectations and goals for ESL;
- to encourage the involvement, participation, and commitment of all school staff in meeting the needs of immigrant, refugee, and visa students in the school;
- to identify the needs of students, their families, and teachers;
- to identify, plan, and implement school-based staff development arising from the local needs identified;
- to encourage the use of local expertise in the school, as well as the support of consultants and other staff within the school system.

A step-by-step guide

Step One: *Form a committee or focus group to*
- conduct a background survey of the school to determine the cultural and linguistic background of the whole school population, including students, teaching and non-teaching staff, office, custodial staff, educational assistants, school community advisors, and so on;
- identify the number of students requiring ESL support;
- identify the programs and services offered in the school to these students and their families.

Step Two: *Plan a series of staff meetings in which teaching and non-teaching staff work in small groups to*
- examine the survey and discuss its implications for the school;
- identify the needs of students requiring ESL support;
- identify the needs of the families of these students;
- identify strategies to meet these needs;
- make suggestions for in-service and professional development;
- share information about the knowledge, skills, and experience of staff so that they can contribute to the professional development of others on staff;
- identify available resources for staff in the school and elsewhere in the system.

Step Three: *Arrange for the focus group to*

- examine the lists of needs and strategies identified by staff;
- prioritize the needs and discuss their implementation;
- plan and set the goals for any in-service needed. Relate these to existing school and Board initiatives;
- discuss the outcomes of the in-service for all staff and plot the path for future improvement.

Reflecting the Principles of Anti-Racist Education

In order to ensure equality of educational opportunity, the school climate must value all cultures equally. Systemic discrimination and bias, often hidden within educational institutions, must be uncovered and challenged.

With your colleagues, consider some of the following questions:

- Does your school have a policy for handling racist behavior? Are racial incidents handled swiftly and firmly by staff?
- Are the same educational opportunities provided for all students, regardless of their language proficiency? Do all students have equal access to the curriculum? Is there a potential for narrowing the curriculum if students are withdrawn into special sections of a subject? Is it discriminatory to mainstream students with no linguistic support? Are students who are learning English allowed to make the same choices as native speakers?
- Are assessment instruments fair to students from various languages and cultures? Should students have the right to be assessed in their first language? At what point is it appropriate to be assessed in the medium of instruction?
- Are the languages and cultural backgrounds of students reflected in the materials and resources selected for library collections and courses of study? Are all materials scrutinized to detect bias?
- Do teachers have positive expectations for all students and give due recognition to the previous education of students from other countries?

- Are there staff members from minority groups to serve as role models? Do any of these hold positions of responsibility in the school?

Extending the Commitment

A continuing review of policy and curriculum will allow staff to air viewpoints and concerns, and make mid-course corrections to a series of planned changes. Administrators can provide a supportive environment by offering sustained staff development opportunities, both during and after school hours. As an example, some school boards and Faculties of Education sponsor courses in teaching ESL for all staff in a school, allowing them to tailor the practica for these courses to the needs of their school, and to the overall needs of the system as a whole. Other courses aim to share the responsibility for teaching new students with a wide variety of Board personnel — curriculum consultants, support staff, and administrators.

System-Wide Initiatives

A supportive school system can make ESL everybody's business by making recommendations about the programming to be provided for its multicultural population. In order to ensure that there is support for students whose progress may be hindered by their linguistic background or their lack of previous educational experience, a school system can undertake a system overview, with ongoing review and evaluation. A system overview that supports the philosophy that all students be provided with equal educational opportunities will disclose:

- the immigration patterns and numbers of students in the system who may require ESL support;
- the registration, reception, assessment, placement, orientation, and transition procedures provided;
- how ESL programs are delivered;
- whether there are adequate staffing and resources for the programs;

- what professional development or in-service opportunities are available for staff.

Political Action

Most school systems are committed to providing programs that will make the lives of their students productive. You have a role in making sure your school board is aware of what is happening in your school, and of the creative programs you have undertaken in response to the changing needs of your school community. You should be proud of your innovative curriculum and policies and keen to publicize them. As well, you can help to formulate and, if necessary, change policy in your school and school system if is not meeting the needs of all your students. In recent years, teachers have become much more willing to articulate current practices and to defend what is good about them. In the future, it may be necessary for you to lobby local authorities and governments for more resources and funding proportionate to the needs of the community you serve. Your goal will be educational justice for all students.

BACKGROUND INFORMATION ON STUDENT POPULATION OF THE SCHOOL

Number of students enrolled in the school _____

Number of students requiring ESL support _____

Major cultural groups in student population _____

Major linguistic groups of students _____

PROGRAMS AND SERVICES AVAILABLE IN THE SCHOOL FOR STUDENTS AND THEIR FAMILIES

ESL classes _____

Life skills programs _____

Special subject classes for ESL _____

Extra-curricular programs _____

Resource room help _____

Peer tutoring services _____

Counselling/Social services _____

Interpreters _____

Parents' Association/Support group _____

Adult ESL classes _____

Adult continuing education classes _____

Recreational programs _____

BACKGROUND SURVEY OF TEACHING AND NON-TEACHING STAFF OF THE SCHOOL

1. What is your job/title/position at the school? _____

2. Were you born in this country?   Yes ____ No ____
   If No, at what age did you come to this country? _____

3. What is your first language? _____

4. What other languages do you speak? _____

5. In your current position, have you been called upon to use a language other than English?   Yes ____ No ____

   If Yes, how often? Regularly __ Occasionally __ Rarely __

6. Have you been invited to share your knowledge of a particular cultural group with your colleagues at the school?
   Yes ____ No ____

7. Would you be willing to act as a resource person to develop awareness among your colleagues of a specific cultural group?
   Yes ____ No ____
   If Yes, which cultural group? _____

8. In your current position, how have you been able to assist second language learners and/or their families?
   _____

9. What specific kinds of training/in-service/professional development would enable you to serve the needs of ESL students and their families more effectively?
   _____
   _____
   _____

10. Additional comments _____
    _____
    _____

Bibliography

Ashworth, Mary. *Beyond Methodology: Second Language Teaching and the Community.* Cambridge, England: Cambridge University Press, 1985.

Benesch, Sarah ed. *ESL in America.* Portsmouth, New Hampshire: Heinemann Educational Books Inc., 1991.

Cummins, J. *Empowering Minority Students.* Scaramento, CA: California Association for Bilingual Education, 1989.

Eisling, John H. *Multicultural Education and Policy: ESL in the 1990's.* Toronto: The Ontario Institute for Studies in Education Press, 1989.

Fullan, M. and Hargreaves, A. *What's Worth Fighting For? Working Together For Your School.* Toronto: Ontario Public School Teachers' Federation, 1991.

Johnson, D. and Johnson, R. *Leading the Cooperative School.* Edina, Minn.: Interaction Book Company, 1989.

Kagan, S. *Cooperative Learning Resources for Teachers.* Riverside, CA: University of California, 1988.

Krashen, Stephen D. "Effective Second Language Acquisition: Insights from Research" in J.E. Alatis, H.B. Altman, P.M. Alatis (eds.) *The Second Language Classroom: Directions for the 1980's.* New York: Oxford University Press, Inc., 1981.

Nelson, Marie Wilson. *Teaching Basic and ESL Writers*. Portsmouth, New Hampshire: Heinemann Education Books Inc., 1991.

Rigg, Pat and Virginia G. Allen (eds.) *When They Don't All Speak English — Integrating the ESL Student into the Regular Classroom*. Urbana, Illinois: National Council of Teachers of English, 1989.